"*Death Does Not End at the Sea* is more than a great first book, it's a mature reworking of contemporary elegy. Gbenga Adesina reconfigures the loss/ghost of his father into odes celebrating vulnerability and personality—as well as Fela Kuti in Versace and a globetrotting James Baldwin. The tender, scrutinizing spirit of Baldwin guides these beautiful meditations on the nature of love and grief. *Death Does Not End at the Sea* is more than a debut, it's a revelation."

—Terrance Hayes, author of *Lighthead*,
winner of the National Book Award for Poetry

"Gbenga Adesina's *Death Does Not End at the Sea* is a requiem for kinship, familial bonds, tethered histories, and splintered branches that always remember their roots. Adesina bridges memory both personal and collective with the migratory movements of global Black life. What results is a poetry in witness and celebration, a tenderness and veneration, a welcome song in our dawn!"

—Matthew Shenoda, author of *Tahrir Suite: Poems*
and *The Way of the Earth*

"*Death Does Not End at the Sea* is a collection from a poet who has matured in voice and craft. Every line quivers with a deft music. The layering of meaning, philosophy/hope, grief, rebirth, ethical questioning, and song is unsurpassed. A major talent and an important voice, Gbenga Adesina has earned every victory in this book, every accolade it will earn, and every moment of luminosity, of which there are many. In this breathtaking work we encounter a poet who carries this tradition with an easy grace. Beautiful."

—Chris Abani, author of *Smoking the Bible*

THE RAZ/SHUMAKER PRAIRIE SCHOONER
BOOK PRIZE IN POETRY

Editor

Kwame Dawes

DEATH DOES NOT END AT THE SEA

GBENGA ADESINA

UNIVERSITY OF NEBRASKA PRESS

Lincoln

The University of Nebraska Press is part of a land-grant institution with campuses and programs on the past, present, and future homelands of the Pawnee, Ponca, Otoe-Missouria, Omaha, Dakota, Lakota, Kaw, Cheyenne, and Arapaho Peoples, as well as those of the relocated Ho-Chunk, Sac and Fox, and Iowa Peoples.

For customers in the EU with safety/GPSR concerns, contact:
gpsr@mare-nostrum.co.uk
Mare Nostrum Group BV
Mauritskade 21D
1091 GC Amsterdam
The Netherlands

LIBRARY OF CONGRESS CATALOGING-IN-PUBLICATION DATA
Names: Adesina, Gbenga, author
Title: Death does not end at the sea / Gbenga Adesina.
Description: Lincoln : University of Nebraska Press, [2025] | Series: The Raz/Shumaker prairie schooner book prize in poetry
Identifiers: LCCN 2025015404
ISBN 9781496244772 (paperback)
ISBN 9781496245854 (epub)
ISBN 9781496245861 (pdf)
Subjects: BISAC: POETRY / African |
LCGFT: Poetry
Classification: LCC PR9387.9 .A341536 D43 2025
LC record available at https://lccn.loc.gov/2025015404

Designed and set in Garamond Premier Pro by Katrina Noble.

For my family, my first chorus. Our chorus will never break apart.

Where is my rest place? Where is my harbor?
Where is the pillow I will not have to pay for,
and the window I can look from that frames my life?

Derek Walcott

We are dreaming all wrong. Who's a stranger? Am I the stranger?

Toni Morrison

CONTENTS

DEATH DOES NOT END AT THE SEA

GLORY

Glory of plums, femur of Glory.
Glory of ferns
on a dark platter.

Glory of willows, Glory of Stag beetles
Glory of the long obedience
of the kingfisher.

Glory of waterbirds, Glory
of thirst.

Glory of the Latin
of the dead and their grammar
composed entirely of decay.

Glory of the eyes of my father
which, when he died, closed
inside his grave,

and opened even more brightly
inside me.

Glory of dark horses
running furiously
inside their own

dark horses.

I

I CARRIED MY FATHER ACROSS THE SEA

He was a child. He was dead.
He was the shaft of a long-tailed astrapia. He was a forest

of bruise. He wore a door on his face.
He wore the black suit

of his wedding. The square pocket
was still full of his vows.

He was light to carry,
his burdens and vows had bled out of him.

He was heavy
with the responsibility of the dead.

What sort of a son
leaves his father

chained to fatherhood?
I lifted and propped him up with my frame.

I measured the length of him with my length.
The feet stuck in sea sand, his weak knees,

his arms gripped my sides.
As the currents rose, the collar on his broken neck

flared into a float.
The gash the surgeon's knife left on his head

became a halo, it signaled in the dark.
I put my nose to his nose.

I put my finger in his mouth.
I tied his IV tubes, now a human gill, around our waists

and swam in the vein
of the water.

"Look," a sphinx in the waves said.
"A son carries a father."

Death is not silence.
It is where I hear you most clearly.

What sort of a son
leaves his father's body

chained to the dark grievance inside the earth?
I carried my father on my back.

I felt the bracing inside his afterlife heart
on the skin of my spine.

He wore his face as a door
he promised to open to me.

He bled
out his vows.

THE PEOPLE'S HISTORY OF 1998

France won the World Cup.
Our dark goggled dictator died from eating

a poisoned red apple
though everyone knew it was the CIA.

We lived miles from the Atlantic.
We watched *Dr. Dolittle, Titanic, The Mask*

of Zorro. Our grandfather, purblind and waiting
for the kingdom of God, sat on a throne in his dark

room, translating Dante.
The Galileo space probe revealed

there was an entire ocean hiding beneath a sheet
of ice in Jupiter's moon.

The Yangtze River in China lost its nerve
and wanted vengeance.

Elsewhere a desert caught fire.
We got a plastic green turtle and named it Sir

Desmond Tutu.
A snake entered our house through the drain

and like any good son, I ran
and hid under the bed.

Google became a thing.
Viagra became a thing.

In July, it flooded at nights and a wind nearly
tore off our roof. I thought God is so in love

with us,
he wants to fill us with himself.

Mother, I saw her through a slit in the door, a glimpse
of amaranth-red scarf and swirling yellow skirt.

She thought no one was looking. She was dancing in a trance
to Fela Kuti. She laughed and clapped

at the mirror. It was the year our house became a house
of boys and girls, and a ghost, our little sister.

Calmaria. That's what the Portuguese called it. When it rained
and the world was suddenly becalmed, we would run

and peel out of the door, waving at the aurora
of birds flitting past in the sky.

We knew one of them, the little one, used to be one of us,
those spectral white egrets.

THE WEDDING

She wore a crown. She wore a white veil.
Beneath the veil, she wore the face of her mother,

a translated story.
She wore a crystal stud on her nose.

She wore droop earrings on her earlobes,
cones of ruby, an alive stone.

Her gown, bridal white, craft of tulle, cathedral.
I lift the veil, your face is my face, mother.

The groom wore a tailcoat, pink begonia
on his chest. His head covered by shreds

of white confetti, feathers of artificial geese.
His head and neckline, his eyes, a painter's eyes

were tilted and affixed to her.
Striped poplar of partial light through the chapel

window cast a ladder on her face. Love is heaven.
But it requires climbing.

It was customary that they should feed each other cake
and heavy honey.

He held a pearl-handled silver cup to her lips.
She drank. He drank.

Something of their vows elongated inside them.

Soon, they will proceed to a small room and anoint
each other arms and necks, each other thighs

and torso with olive oil in preparation for beauty,
not death. Soon, one will wrap the other in a white

shroud for burial as it was written from the beginning.
I whisper to them from the future: Please, pray for light.

For now, they lean close and kiss, she cups his face
with her hands.

A priest burns incense and blue myrrh
behind a raised altar.

As witness, a child dressed in a brilliant purple cassock
plays an unfinished violin.

SURRENDER

A mercy puts a thing
on my palm and
it is my childhood.
Its tiny endless moth city,
its rind like grace
or tenderness
or sorrow

∞

In the red brick room, my father cries.
His cries are small, lonely animals.
I carry them with me
like an inheritance.

∞

Once, I ran out
of a room
because the song
on the radio
was a fist
in the nook of my neck.
I stood
on the street
quietly weeping.
Though when a woman said to me:
"Child, are you well?"
I said it was the waters
within me that wanted to
make themselves known.

∞

Some nights are like that. They do not let you go
until they have broken into the secret July in your heart where you hide all things.

∞

All I wanted
was to be home,
so I dipped myself
under the earth.
By which I mean
I entered the subway station.

∞

It was there I heard him.
A man that was also a sound.
His face was like the face of John Coltrane.
He was singing. Tree
branches broke
inside his voice.

∞

There was, in his chorus, the quietude of a thing that was coming to an end.
This song he was singing, he said it was not a dirge.
Though he sang it to a thing that was dying.

∞

Which in a way
was the kind of song
my father sang
as he lay dying.
My father said
his song was not a dirge.
Though he sang it
to a thing that was dying
in himself.
He said son:

my song is a joy.
But a joy with sharp knives.

∞

So, my laughter is a thing with a sharp edge.
And my joy a trembling.

∞

This man I saw,
his locks of hair
which ran down to his neck
were the
borders
of a country inside him.
And the sound he made
was the secret language
of a nation unto which
immigrants were called.

∞

It was as though I had sliced through the ocean and arrived here,
only to run into my childhood.

And I did not want to make myself open. But I was made open
for certain songs do not ask your permission.

∞

I raised my hands
and moved toward him,
naked before the song.
I said:
Dear Music, dear childhood.
Take me.
Take me.

IN SEARCH OF JAMES BALDWIN IN PARIS

He taught me how to see and how to trust what I saw.
                                —*Baldwin on Beauford Delaney*

I

We were gazing at Rembrandt's "Philosophers in Meditation" at the Louvre.
Father and son. I was thirty-five. Half the age of my father when he died.
My son was five and had no past other than the past of our ancestors.
My father loved the soft pulp of avocados and loved to whistle. He loved maps
and drew them on the backs of notebooks and newsprints and regaled me with
the names of exotic cities: "Do you know *Bujumbura*? Do you know
Turin and *Verona*? One day, I'll take you to *Marseille*."
But a heavy, invisible duty held him bound to a small place. He never
traveled. So, I vowed the eyes of my son would see the world.
In the museum, transfixed before the painting, I craned my neck to the left.
My son craned his neck to the left too. I could not turn my gaze from the painting.
I secretly wanted to see with my son's eyes. Son, what do you see?
In the painting, the low yellow light of an invisible sun rises
through a window like the lights of certain plants which rise
delicately from the roots and stems and stain the fruits with ripeness.
A curved oak stair bifurcates the room. The deep vellum brown of the
wooden steps are grainy as if to depict private dust. A small hatch door
sits underneath the stairs. A priest sits, hands clasped in meditation.
An old woman reaches for a log in the fire mantle or an illuminated manuscript.
My son was looking intently. Son, what do you see? What do the colors say to you?

II

On the Metro over the Pont Rouelle Bridge, I looked
at the train glass smeared with grease, human fog, and breath
and in the mirrored profiles of heads, I couldn't find my face.
I panicked. I looked beside me and at the throng of commuters
and couldn't find my son. A wave of black birds crashed against my chest.
I felt a clog in my throat. It was a dream.
I woke up and he was on his iPad beside me on our bed
at an apartment in the 2nd arrondissement, playing Peppa Pig.
Outside the window, I could hear the patter of rain.
From here, if I looked, I could see the house where
Baldwin wrote *Giovanni's Room*.
When my son was three, he couldn't sleep unless
his nose was close to my arm or neck as if he needed to inhale me.
It made me feel alive. I would put my ears to his chest and listen
to the rise and fall of his chest. I was trying to listen to his dreams.
If I wanted to sleep, I would tie the edge of his cloth
to the edge of my cloth to form a Klemheist knot, as if to say: There
was no world in which I would let him disappear from me.

III

We had gone to see the city's oldest church—the Church
of Saint-Germain-des-Prés
There, a priest prayed the prayer of shipwreck for me,
not as in death or ruin, lament or pathos, but how
a grain of barley must first sink into a brief rot
so that the fragrant and deeper life inside it
might be made manifest.
I knelt and my son knelt beside me.
Everywhere we went, my son and I, our blackness,
was a cloak, a musk, and a halo. We were invisible.
Yet we reflected like silver on all surfaces.
This set my son free—he
laughed and hopped, he waved and winked
at strangers. At a park, he wanted a tiny dog
to lick his face and tried to kiss
a barracuda fish through a glass aquarium.
People stopped us to say how beautiful
he was. A woman asked to touch his hair—
it made me greatly afraid.
The law of physics said it was my sacred
duty to protect his fragile bones.
Someone offered to take our picture.
I watched a shadow deepen and spread
across the marbled blue sky.
In the photograph, I held my son
close and would not let go.

IV

I couldn't go to a jazz club because I couldn't
afford a babysitter, so we are sitting on the carpet
in an apartment in the 2nd arrondissement.
I'm playing Coltrane's *A Love Supreme* for my son.
The trumpet is a door. The plucked harp strings.
The drums lead a procession. Piano keys
that are lights jouissance on the surface of a summer lake
Son, what do you hear?
Do you hear the trumpet's groan, which really,
is Coltrane's desperate keening in a language
of sweet, tortured wind? Or the sermon of his father
who was a preacher. Son, you are my sermon.
Baldwin's broken father was a preacher. But his sermon
was bitter. When young Baldwin ran—he said *I couldn't breathe*—
to France and later to Turkey and Switzerland, he traveled
with his stash of Bessie Smith, Billie Holiday, Aretha Franklin,
and Nina Simone and his mother's voice. Music was his sanctified church.
My son's face, the riddle and mystery of my mother's face
in his face as he listens to me sing is my psalm, my holy church.

BRIEF HISTORY

1960

The night the flag of the British Empire came down
in my country, the cry of a mottled wolf was heard in the wild.
In a monastery near the delta, a woman
saw stone doves flapping their wings
in the dark and panicked, but it was the white cenotaphs of Christian
missionaries.
In a coastal town that abuts the lagoon
and the "Point of No Return" a priest, a returned slave,
prayed in groans and translated scriptures.
In a long house with a warren of rooms, a sculptor tore a page
from a book of maps in her dream and made a paper ship
she named *Amistad*, a gift, she whispered to her daughter
in that dream, a gift from the ghosts, for they too are citizens.
That night, street sweepers, some of whom
were shepherd poets, leaned their mouths close to the shrubs
and star apple trees of their villages, and chanted as they swept, believing
that the earth had ears and could be made tender
by miracle speech. That night, a young playwright dreamt
and saw the swaying dance of a forest.
In a tower with a colonial balustrade, young
soldiers, among them future dictators, slept and rehearsed in their dreams
the future deaths they would bring.
They believed cruelty was their destiny.
All the families had sons they would give
to the war, so they prayed for daughters.
A country made for ruins. There was no country.
In a grove of spruce, a widow, before her child
was lowered into the grave in the dark, closed
his eyelids in the coffin, said, "Hurry on now.

Go meet the King." It was a dream.
In a deeper dream, in a rotunda of plums,
voices were heard among tupelos, the laughter of spirit children.
A garment maker, my grandfather, muttered
in his sleep, "Oh God, what a century,
what a century."
A black hawk lifted above a white cliff
and disappeared into the blue wine-jar of heaven.
It was a dream. There was no heaven.
This is the history of the night my mother was born.

THE LOVERS OF MODENA

Your hands in the small
place of my bones,

shore of skin
slow furl.

Lord, such delicious
ruin.

Love's vast colony of hunger.
The map lines crackle, they run

in my maple wood veins.
I would that you know

what is hidden is what is broken
is what is holy.

The mouth, remember,
is red clay.

Time,
rock, weathering

rock, lie here with me
in the dark.

We are the histories
of dust.

I speak to you from my flesh to your flesh:

My loss is a loss with doors.

It opens.

COMA

A SEQUENCE

1

i

When the call came, it was my mother.
There was a strange velocity on her tongue.
Time was both beginning and at the end
in her mouth.
She was saying: "Come. Please, come quick.
It's about your father's body."

ii

I ran. I ran
with the horses
and the horses' scar of birth
inside me.
I ran
with the wing trembling
inside my name toward
that room of death.

iii

At the door
of the ICU we,
my brothers, sisters,
and I were stopped
and given nose masks
before we were allowed inside.
The dreams of those who lay dying, we were told,
was a thing one could inhale.

iv

The shock of iodine
to the nose,
smell of hospitals,
dull
fluorescent lights.
A cluster of faces
surrounded
a body covered
in a blue
paper gown.
His head was fresh
with
a wound,
a red gash.
He lay so still.
Even his mother's name
must have been frozen
inside him
I saw then his chest
rising and falling,
rising and falling.
He was breathing.
Father! You are alive.
I moved toward
him,
and saw, no, it was the tube
connected to him
that was breathing
inside him.
I fell to my knees.

v

My mother put her mouth to my father's ear,
Christ to Lazarus, and said, "Wake up. I command you.
Wake up.
You belong to me.
Your body, clove, rosemary, bread,
it belongs
to me. Rise, on this third day.
I know your name. Wake up
Please, do not fail me."

vi

On the fourth day, we formed a circle
around his bed
and began to read to him.
The brain, Ornette Coleman
teaches us,
is a conversation.
He loved the language
of the epics.
There was a book I had been secretly
writing for years. It was a book of silence.
The silence between father and son.
I held it in my hands now. A small offering.
He responded with silence.

vii

I went out to the hospital corridor
and then to a nearby orchard.
I saw a family of black pileated woodpeckers and their crowns in a veil of trees.
They circled the air and dove in their black-white choir robes.
When they flew, their small red crowns flared open
into small wings or wounds attached to their heads.
They shot through the trees in a ritual of seasons.
It was as if they had a book or a testament in their beaks.
Their destiny, simply, was beauty.

viii

Later that evening, in a quiet voice, the doctor said: "I'm sorry. Your father is now brain dead."

Father, is a book a stone of silence?

x

Father, this silence is a prairie country. This silence
is the silence of hospital sheets.
The silence is of IV tubes and veins.
The silence is the silence of what
is dappled invisibly by a body
that is no longer human but not yet a ghost. The silence is in your
lungs but it has lodged in my throat.
Silence, can you hear me? The silence is of lime,
and kraal stones. The silence is the silence, not of a shadow
but of light buried under a stone.
The silence is the silence
of hands. *Hands, hands, can you hear me?*
The silence is the silence of broken ribs.
The silence is the silence of the head,
shorn and shaven. The silence is silence of a bandage wrapped
tight around what is sunken, what is fallen in the gait of the head
Head, head can you hear me?
The silence is silence of blood.
Blood, blood, can you hear me?

2

i

When I try to remember my father's last act
in our house, I remember nothing,
but prayer.
He knelt before his wife, my mother,
who placed
a hand on his head.
His children surrounded him.
He said: Darkness
wants to take my body.
Please, pray for me.

ii

Once in a dream, I saw my father through
a keyhole in his glass heaven.
I thought now that he was dead, to whom did he pray?
His favorite song in life was still his favorite song in death.
"Glory," He sang. Among the choir of the dead.
"Glory. Glory. Glory. Glory," they sang.

iii

At first, my youngest brother did not see our father's spent body.
He was too young, my mother said. He's to be protected
from the news of our extinction.
At the funeral, before the white swaddle was lowered into the earth,
we went to look at it for the last time.
My father's nostrils, ears, and mouth were stuffed with white cotton
balls as if to prevent whatever residual language remained inside him
from spilling out. I felt a presence slip into the room.
The presence came close and stood beside me.
It was my youngest brother. He had snuck into the room.
He was seeing his father's body in death for the first time.
He gasped. He held on to my hands.
I felt his body tremble.
We both began to weep.

My father, it's important to mention, could not dance.
He refused to acknowledge this. In fact, he declared himself
a masterful dancer. Fela Kuti in Versace.
He couldn't sing either. This he admitted,
though it never stopped him from trying to go on far
fetched solos when the family sang together.
He would sometimes dance for us.
He would spread out his arms in a wide span
as in the glide of a white stork. He would then tilt his upper
body forward and start to dance. A strange dance-walk.
In the heat of the dance, when the music was deep inside
him, he would start to stamp his feet on the ground. His olive oiled
head glistening with sweat, the small hollow cups of his shoulders,
the ridge line of his chest. He would place his left hand gingerly
on the small of his back and the right one on his forehead.
When he had achieved what he believed was a perfect rhythm,
he would pause to laugh, the laughter of pleasure, and applaud
himself: "Ah, look at that. Won't join me?
Look at that. Wonderful! Merciful God."

v

Once in a dark room,
five brothers and sisters
danced the dance of their dead father.
The darkness in the room was a private question.
We sat at first in stillness.
Then one brother began to sing a song
in the father's voice.
Another sister began to mumble in the father's silence.
The song, the voice, and the silence were a choral unity.
Slowly, like a dirge, we stood up
and began to dance to the silence.
I stood up and began to dance
to what was hidden
in the silence.
I bent my body, my inheritance,
I spread my arms
into a *V*, as in that of white storks,
their instinct and ritual of migrations.
I danced till I could feel my name,
which means light and lifted wings,
move inside me.
I danced till my olive oiled head
glistened,
and water ran down the small hollow
cups of my shoulders
into the ridge line of my chest
as if to sink
through my veins
and water the tender
roots inside me.
On the wall, the silhouettes of brothers and sisters

danced and moved from solitude to solitude.
They held hands.
I gave myself to the chorus of the living,
the dead and the unborn.
I'm my father when I'm dancing.

I had vowed the eyes of my son would see the world.
The fruits—Bergeron apricots, Calville Blanc apples, and peaches—
that grow here carry the terroir of the soil, and in their seeds
they carry delicately a sweetness that though it springs
from the mulch of death transcends decay.
When Baldwin came here in the '70s, exhaustion lived
like a worm in his breastbone.
At the funerals of his friends—Medgar (1963), Malcom (1965),
Martin (1968)—he wore the black suit he had worn to their weddings.
He sprung a white handkerchief from his pocket
which fluttered slightly and trembled like a blind dove
to comfort their widows who themselves were daughters
of widows. He fled his country.
I took my son to see the palimpsest of the house
he bought in Saint-Paul de Vence: a seventeenth-century stone house
with twelve rooms, a rose garden, and a terrace from where he could smell
and inhale the salted breeze of the Mediterranean.
He believed all salts and all oceans carried a whiff of his ancestors.
In that breeze and castle, he danced and laughed
and partied. He hosted Miles Davis and Ella Fitzgerald.
But when he slept, he cried in his sleep, and a white horse
with black hooves ran in a circle in his dreams.
In those dreams: Malcom and Martin and Medgar
were ruddy children running around in a field of yellow butterflies
and they were asking him to come join them since
tiredness was a burden only for the living
and they had found a strange rest at the other end of the bullets.
When he startled awake, he cried and laughed and danced
some more in the breeze and salt and staggered with a bottle of rum
to the window. The villagers were aloof in those first years, but he won
them over with his charm. I held the hand of my son and felt a great quiet

descend on me as we walked the grounds of the small village.
On the porch of a restaurant waiting for a meal of *pan bagnat*,
suddenly excited, my son decided to break
dance to a song in his head like he was some Prince
of *Purple Rain*. He stood, bobbed, twirled his hands
and slid into a moonwalk. I was nervous. We were in the public.
I wanted to stop him. But I heard laughter and claps and a clink of glasses,
and a gaggle of French and English from the patrons
who were applauding him. A bead of sweat dilated down my neck.
It was relief. Nothing would break our delicate bones today.

II

*

The bottom of the sea is cruel.

—Hart Crane

We know these beautiful boats have death in them.

—Edna O'Brien

DEATH DOES NOT END AT THE SEA

1

On the Mediterranean.

The Chorus is the muscle memory of the sea.

i

On the sea, the prayer is not to the whorl scarf
of waves. The prayer is to the fitful sleep of the dead.
Look. You must look. You cannot
look away. Their bodies, their torsos, their mouths curve darkly
and arrow down into the water. What do you call a body
of water made of death and silence?

ii

Look.   A clutch of stars,   a clutch of blue-white stars in a sky above

dead white water.   A scene from prehistory,   except it's our history

and   we are the cast of ghosts   in it.

Look. We are on a raft on the ocean, the Raft of Medusa. We are at the edge

or   middle   of   nowhere, a geography of melancholy, where

       no hand   of   father   or   nation reach   out

to   claim   us.

We   have   been

left stranded   in the middle   of the earth.
Men   and   women, and children   on rubber boats.
A helicopter circles us. History circles us.

We raise   our hands   above   our

heads   to say we come in peace.
We raise our hands   in surrender,   or in prayer to a strange God.
History is a strange god.

When suddenly   a ballast   of stormy water   hits the hull   of the boat,

in the panic   of drowning,   I heard   a wail
I thought,   for a moment,   was my mother's.
The language   in which those   who drown   cry out   is inside us.

iii

On this shore, all the objects carry
an animal silence. The objects know
something, but they refuse to talk to us.
A yellow scarf. A wrinklet of black
beads, the phone of a dead woman
ringing in the white sand. There is a
purple shirt in deep sleep on the
shore. The wind wakes it, but it falls
back to its slumber and decay.
There is a bleached photograph
on the ground. In it a man smiles.
There is someone else's hands
on his shoulder, in embrace, but
where there should be a face, there is emptiness.

iv

So, I'm writing toward your face: my beloved, my disappeared,
your ivory, your lightening.
I'm writing toward our choral country, our blighted
country where the land is stung by the graves
of children,
where something trembles and sighs like a ladder
but does not lead to heaven and does not lead to earth.

Chorus:

The children of God are upon frightened waters
and God being hunger, God being the secret grief of salt,
moves among his people and does not spare them.
The children of God are upon frightened waters.

2

[Solitary ensemble or a cast of ghosts]

i

Who is this man I glimpse on the shore, in a photograph
of immigrants rescued from a capsized boat on the coast of Italy?
They carry him like a seed that must not touch the earth.
The rescue workers wear nose masks to remain in a separate air from him,
a separate eternity. He sits on a wheelchair. The coast guards
are bent toward him to ask a question or as though to bow
in obeisance to his suffering.
His face, on that rescue vessel, is ghostly, haunted. He looked
like someone who, in another life, carried water polished
pebbles in his pockets and told stories because his assigned task
and inheritance on earth was to be the memory of his people.
They ask him to pose, smile for a photograph.
When he looked at the camera he looked as if he was thirsting
for light.

I met her at a market in Marrakesh.
We began a first tentative dance with our eyes,
then whispers. She found my mouth. We had different tongues.
I spoke English, she spoke a deeper tongue.
She sang her story. She said this is my song: the song of old vows,
song of old stones, song of plumes and gust of wind, song
of prophets in red dusts. Song of the great God of reward, God
of humiliation. For bread, she carried heavy things
across borders. She tied a tiny phone to her waist,
someday the daughter the sea took away might call.
She said she does not delete the phone numbers
of the dead. To fortify herself, she attends funerals
and comforts those like herself: the fathers and mothers of ghosts.
To the dead, she says,
"At least you have nothing heavy to carry now
but your own spirit."

And who was that man I met on the coast of Tajura, east of Tripoli?
He had been held and tortured in a narrow cell in Libya.
But he was out now. "All my suffering," he said, smiling, "are in the past."
As if torture can be banished from the memory of a body.
He was at the shore planning his next move, full of maps.
Spreading out his arms, he said, "These waters
are the waters of my fathers. The waters
of my mothers. These waters are the waters of my intimacy;
the waters of my estrangement.
You see, I was born on the small island of Gorée, by the mouth of the sea.
As a child I fished for shells, herrings, and salmons but really what I was
fishing for was the ghost of my father. The men of my family leave
on these waters. Some never return.
Tomorrow, I too shall set sail. It's my destiny."

iv

Look. You cannot look away. Clouds. And on the face of the clouds,
fury. On the face of a dark ocean, a migrant dinghy undulates. Let us name
it *Jesus of Lubbeck*. It's empty. A moment ago, before you arrived
on this page, it was sinking. Half of its passengers are underwater.
They belong to gravity now. The other half are on board a rescue vessel.
The children, mostly in white swaddle, were rescued first, lifted out
of the water like an offering of doves. The adult survivors sit on a metal floor,
their hands shivering. There is a stony quiet. Death like a strange wind
has moved through them. The men and women huddle and breathe together
as though learning how to breathe again.
Then the women begin to kneel and bow to something in the distance.
The men kneel behind the women and bow to whatever it is the women
are bowing to. They breathe, they cry out, language returns to them.
They have survived. They have not survived.

3

i

What the Gravedigger Says

I dig and build passage graves shaped like upturned boats.
I build stone cathedrals through which the dead tunnel to heaven.
I command the dead to swim.
Not even the great animals of grief who like us bury their dead,
the mute swans, and tundra wolves,
and Borneo elephants, not even them can smell the dead through twelve inches
of soil. It's why it's called burial.
Burial: byrgan *from Old English meaning "to conceal, to shelter."*
I shelter the dead.
Burial: bergan *from Old Saxon meaning "to hide, to protect"*
I protect the dead.
Do you know orphan elephants who watched their mothers
killed in the forest, wake up in the morning, even as adults, screaming?
It's the bones of the dead singing inside you.
The dead, being dead, sing in their graves
and their bones inside us become a flute. It is why we
cry. It's the bones of the dead singing inside you.
Did you cry? Have you cried?
The dead, you ask, are they not thirsty in their small boxes?
Why do you think
your father died with his mouth open?
He knew even in the grave God would send rain.
Digging is my prayer.
I measure the silence and the O of mouth
around the silence. I dig to arrive at grief.
To equal births must be equal deaths,
I dig to arrive at the transition.

But on these waters, this boat,
though there are deaths, I'm jobless.
The sea is the grave and the gravedigger.

What the Apothecary Says

My name is Deuteronomy Oniworobo. I'm a healer.
I make potions that control bleedings and swellings,
And the serious burn of being born
on the wrong side of history or ocean.
the wrong side of a country or a language.
I know you lost a country, lost a language, you lost your name.
I repair the lesions of the spirit
and deep cuts reignited in winter,
The black gash of departure, a form of history.
When I work, I feel where the tension in your
veins tightens. History elongates in my fingers.
I hear the friction of the dead,
the swish of their thighs
as they walk in their heavy lace. I repair the contours
of flesh where your muscle twitches in your sleep.
My emergency care is salt.
There are wounds inside which you'll find glass, gravel, splinter
of chalk, exile, or shame. I extract the stasis of ruins that gather inside
a name when it has been mispronounced for too long.
I extract the teeth rust sunk in the neck of your mother's wedding gown.
The one she kept inside a forgotten metal box. Her beauty is history
now. But she has not forgotten her dance.
I know the night is a refrain. I know there is a winter you will never forget.
I know there are hands you allowed to touch your body
but did not allow to touch your name.
Sometimes, a child makes it on this journey but is marked by the exile
of the mother.
Your loneliness is your share of the loneliness of your people. I wake up in the
morning and play the music of my father and mother to remind myself that my
spirit is not an orphan in the world. Our lives are not tragic, but our country

is tragic. Famine teaches the tongue to never again trust the surface of water.
On the sea, there are things I saw from which my eyes have not returned.
I carry always with me my black bag of cures. For sudden fevers of shame
that comes with exile, I prescribe a drop of dew on the tongue.
For dark memories, I prescribe a chew of ash or forgetting.
But my love, I should tell you there is no cure for longing.

What the Hairdresser Says

My name is Medusa Onidiri.
On this boat, I place the head gently on my lap,
I butter my fingers with shea and begin to work my hands
like a visitation into the roots and tangle of hair.
I rub argan oil (and the oil from burdock roots and nettle leaves) with my palm
into the scalp. I comb, I caress.
In mammals, the hair is the first portal of resurrection.
We are the only species whose hair does not become fossil.
I comb, I caress. I trace the hairlines with my fingers
and section the hair into small rows, small bridges.
I braid, slowly, tenderly, like one who braids memory.
I arrive at the final stems of hair like the veins of a family tree.
I plait and braid facing the north, slowly, tenderly, I'm telling a story.
I anoint the head with oil.
And does it matter that the body on my lap,
my sister, is pale and unmoving, dead on this journey, this sea,
you think even the dead do not desire beauty?

4

i

[*Love Poems at the Mouth of the Sea*]

You think
We do not know love?

She says,
the first time

he ever spoke to me, he said:
"Your lips, they are the plums of God."

I was watching him swim, his hands, his torso,
how he sliced through the water with such public gentleness.

As I watched him, I suddenly knew
his past was heavy and unfinished inside him.

Because he was kind to the water,
I knew he would be kind to me.

He gave me his mother's ring.
At our wedding, I wore

a blue dress
and a crown of forsythia.

For our vows, he gave me promises he dug out
of white sand, or words he stole it from a poet.

He says:

I met her inside a blue scarf. I met her inside a train of mist.
I met her inside my thirst.
We were dancing at a club, carefree like small sweaty gods.
I was shy at first. I danced in circles around her.
Then, I praised the cleft and claw of her mouth, red salmon.
Her yellow-red shawl, her fingers.
I praised her teeth, small white serrations.
I praised the moon of her lips.
Then she whispered to me:
My name is inside your mouth.
Let me teach you how to say it.

iii

Look, a couple is getting
married on the shore.
They are waiting to cross the sea.
But here at this hour, they wait and stand
before each other with vows. There is no hurry.
Love, remember,
is heaven but it requires climbing.
They met on the journey.
They both have no countries
now, but their own imagination.
They do not speak
the same language, but they share a tongue.
Their geography, if they have one, is a cleft of lips,
archipelago of thighs and entangled legs.
They say to each other: Mouth of sea, sea of mouth, kiss me.
Torso of water,
come alive, come alive,
inside me.

iv

On a different shore, on a different day, a man is bent on his knees, wailing
at the waters. He slaps his hand on the wet sand and rough-cut stones
the way one might fight a brother. He grabs the shirt of the sand
and wrestles with the earth. Here, the stones carry the island's
low cry inside them. A landlocked grief.
They say the man was newlywed. They say his love had the face of Absalom.
They said if the sea had any shame it wouldn't swallow such a beautiful man.
Now, their vows are inside the water.
The man claws at the sand. He wails: *Ocean, Ocean,*
you owe me a body. Ocean, give me back my lover.

5

i

[flute-bone of a ghost childhood]

For every child born in exile, there is an alternative childhood, a ghost
childhood trapped inside a box back home.
On the sea, the children invent playmates
out of pelicans and herons. They point to the flying black gravities
overhead and giggle. The birds scarf through the sky, dive and leave their
shadows on the plexiglass-skin of water. A child laughs,
claps, tickled by the sword of shadows, sword of wind
that clash like waves on the face of the sea.
There is no metaphor for the drowning of a child.

ii

There is a child here whose protest is against memory.
She has crossed the ocean with her mother,
they are shivering and waiting for her father, two days now, they are waiting.
The ocean splits families. But you know that.
They are waiting and shivering for a father
the mother knows would never arrive. The mother knows
the lungs of the living are ropes joined at the end to the lungs of the dead.
I once heard: The dead who drown at sea do not show their faces
when they return to us in dreams.
In her dreams, she calls his name, but he turns his back and does not face her.
Yet, she keeps talking to his ghost and keeps calling his name.
How to explain this notion in which death felt to her like a short errand from
which return was promised? How to explain this to her child?
As if death was a quick trip to the marketplace.
She holds her child gently and says to her: *It's a brief death.*
Your father has gone on a brief death. He'll soon be back.

iii

Here now, the child whose childhood
fell, tongue first into the water.
Here now, all our enlightenments,
all our futures the anguish
of water swallowed. Darwish, pray for us, your descendant
is a wraith upon the waters. Walcott, please, do not leave us.
Nazim Hikmet, this child has your face.

6

i

[Lights of the World]

They spread out on the shore. Men and women. A TV crew speaks to them.
One held a copy of Derek Walcott's *Omeros*. They are preparing to cross
the Mediterranean. They speak of torture in their countries, torture
in the desert, torture in narrow cells fine citizens of the world paid for.
Now, they are at the mouth of the sea. They are waiting for a sign,
a voice, a benediction to make them wade into the water,
and cross into promise. One had small puffs of hair, like black islands
on her head. Another dyed his hair blue: the color of the flower that grew
like a thorn on his mother's grave.

ii

Sighted on the sea:

an upsurge of lightning

a Saturn of stones

a lamentation of dark
plumes

a trove of fish-beings

a cast of aliens

iii

On the sea, an old sailor once said to me, *you carry your dead inside you*
You carry your dead as you move toward the light of foreign cities.
Your dead, they pray inside you.
Your dead they pray for you to reach the light. The lights of Valencia. Lights
of Palermo. Lights of Malaga. Lights of strange heavens. The lights
from a distance, he said, look like strange fruits.
When you see the lights, he said, smiling now. *You breathe, you sigh. There is death*
between you and the lights, but for now you breathe, you sigh. You pray. You believe.

iv

On the sea, prayer.
The voices lift, they rise,
the voices rise, they lift
The voices rise and lift inside you and knock their heads of waves
on rocks and stones of denudations.
The fruit of ocean is ocean.

v

The fruit of ocean is ocean.
Rocks and stones of destinations.
The voices rise and lift inside you and knock their heads of waves.
The voices rise, they lift.
The voices lift, they rise.
On the sea, prayer.

Chorus:

The children of God are upon frightened waters
And God being hunger, God being the secret grief of salt
Moves among his people and does not spare them.
The children of God are upon frightened waters.

7

One of the men said to the TV crew:
My name nah Leviticus. I dey feel the wind of Spain.
Spain dey call my body, I go enter
Spain. I dey feel the wind. I go become
better somebody. Hunger dey catch
my mouth. But for my heart, I be prince.
I go be Prince of Spain.

III

IN SEARCH OF JAMES BALDWIN IN ISTANBUL

I

We went to the apartment in Taksim Square where in the middle of a party
he had typed the last sentence of *Another Country* and wrote *The Fire Next Time*.
We went to a town on the coast of the Black Sea where he toured his play in Turkish.
We went to his flat in the four-story Ulcer Apartment between the German
and Japanese embassies in Istanbul, where he hosted Marlon Brando and Alex Haley,
unbeknownst to him, an avenue of spies.
We went to the famous Park Hotel where he drank, laughed, and mingled
with diplomats, intellectuals, dissidents, and insomniac poets.
There they said, he once met a flaneur who owned a grey parrot
which cussed only in French. He kissed a violinist who claimed
he was a descendant of Flaubert. At the hotel bar, he would climb the bar stool and sing
like Billie Holiday, then like Nina Simone, to applause and laughter.
The FBI had kept a file on him for decades.
From the terrace of his apartment in Ebe Hanim, it was said, he could see
the Bosphorus, the passage between the Black Sea
and the Mediterranean. The sea, blue with rage and mist
and framed by the peak of the Greater Ararat Mountains.
Something ancient in the light knew his name.
Every morning when he woke up and he looked out to the sea,
He saw American naval ships, white and menacing, circling, circling.

II

I had vowed the eyes of my son would see the world
I wanted to be faithful to his face. It was a form of prayer.
Ambient light was my tool.
In the Basilica Cistern, south of the Hagia Sophia,
ancient Roman columns behind us, I knelt and looked
at him through the camera's aperture. He was pouting,
then smiling, making a mischievous face.
At the press of the shutter, this slice of hour
would become a float of ice frozen into an image
alive and eternal with all my longing and fear.
In 1965, Sedat Pakay took a photograph of Baldwin
in a Turkish tea garden.
In that photograph, I love most his mouth, his lips around
the spear tip of the hookah hose
aspirating, not vapor, but prophecy.
I love his ring adorned hands, one
placed in the middle and the other
at the base, curled around the stem
of the pipe. I love his hooded
eyes slanted downward in pleasure,
rest, and release. I love the dark blue
fish-eyed button on his long collared
cavalry twill jacket and the button
hole, brilliant like the birth scar of a navel.
I love the silver tray and the glass thimbles
and the Turkish teacups facing the east.
I love his black suede shoes, laced
in a cross lock.
I love the man beside him, they do not talk,
they do not hold hands. Their silence
is an extension of their beauty.
I love the pack of cigarettes before him, unopened,
austere like exile.

I love the linden tree which grows in the
middle of the tea shop.
And because these are wise people, no
one had thought to cut down the tree.
Son, I do not want you to be cut down.
I want you to grow wild and brilliant like a tree in Istanbul.
I clicked, he rose, levitated.

III

I had vowed the eyes of my son would see the world.
On the Galata Bridge, I placed him on my shoulders,
so he could see further than I could.
A ghost of the bridge was built in the sixth century
and right before the fall of Constantinople in the fifteenth century,
a bridge of ships was built across the glistening estuary.
Baldwin first here came in 1961. On another leg in 1969, he lived
with Beauford Delaney and a Martinique lover on the Bosphorus.
He came here for peace. What was he running from?
Son, what do your eyes see? The holy spears of white minarets rose
from the great mosques. Ottoman domes and the imperial Topkapi Palace
gleamed in the distance. Ferries left foamy trails on the river,
and around us tourists jostled each other and went past trinket stalls
and spice markets. A pigeon landed on my shoulder and my son called
it his sister. Once, in a fever dream of such stunning darkness that I gasped
for air, I dreamt I offered my son a packet of KitKats, and when he tried
to take it, his left arm had been amputated. I woke up crying.
On the bridge, fishermen held taut lines and rods over the ancient railing.
At night, the fishing rods light up like the fingers of God stretching
down into the blue water.

ALL OF THE LIGHTS

Consider then the thirteen white geese
I saw wandering the cloister at the Barcelona
Cathedral. They wandered over the crypts
of saints, their footfalls audible to none
but themselves, unaware they were
in a sanctuary. They were aware though, I sensed,
that they are made in the image of a white clay
of grace, brilliant ripeness and stillness, movement
and evolution: the slender flute of feathers and reticulate
tarsi, named as they were by the first Adam
for a bright flash he saw in his dream.
Medieval thinkers called their sacred intuition *estimativa*.
They were here before Saint Augustine.
They'll be here long after my son and I are gone.
Praise them.

CITIZEN

The only citizenship I have was given to me
by the Brooklyn trees. The trees of heaven, now ghost trees;
the trees of Canarsie: little-leaf lindens, silver maples, Norway
maples, and their little ship of seeds like ships on the Atlantic.
Or their paired tinted samaras which have wings and
thus love to spiral and flutter down to the soil in the autumn
gardens where I sometimes sit and try to listen
to the labor of aquifers underground, the groan of seeds.
My sister who died and is now underground must be one of those seeds.
The white seeds, milky and deciduous, grow up to feed
Carolina wrens, Buteo hawks and laughing gulls, these birds
of Brooklyn are my companions when I sleep and dream
that I'm singing in my sister's voice,
or that I'm a bird of paradise, high and mauve above a mountain,
gliding over a blue marina, and in that dream I have on my head a crown
of fuchsia, and on my feet the bronze
hooves of white horses, the animals of grief.

Once, in the slice of the dark, returning
from the day's labor, with rose apples in my knapsack, and suddenly remembering
something funny my sister had once said, I laughed
in the dark and blessed myself. Then flush with images of how we
used to climb trees together as children, and knowing that I'm invisible
in this city of gilded harbors anyway, I thought,
though I did not do it, I thought I might climb the bark and silk of this maple tree
I saw and jostle with black ants and vine dust, and go higher and higher,
as in my childhood until I reached the dome of the tree.
And from that high up, look toward the ports and islands and tidal estuaries
of the city and see them as silver constellations held together by a finger of darkness;
Or toward the leafy cloud of the Botanical Garden
where goldenrods, asters and canna lilies sleep in midnight sap

and await resurrection by light. Perhaps, my sister is only asleep.

Or toward the bay of the Hudson, near the Little Red Lighthouse,

where the Atlantic meets the shore, and see my ancestors rise as mist from the ocean.

I thought I might look from my tree and see the mossy acres of Hart Island,

that burial ground of strangers and citizens, where all those we've lost

are under the white dwarf stars of headstones. The spectral multitude.

As if while we slept, the graves, on their own, began

to spread from plot to plot, multiplying all over the face of the earth.

It is not true that I praise the dead. I merely ask them to teach me their song.

116TH STREET

Over a pauper king's feast of sesame bagels, egg,
and bad coffee at a cafe, I'd people-watch
to perfect the architecture of my gaze

in the city of cool, money, ghosts, and ghostly rivers.
I tried to hold my face like Miles (Davis),
it didn't work, I tried Charlie (Parker), it didn't work either,

then I settled for pre-fame Basquiat. Broke, baby faced, and obscure.
I was the nameless protagonist
in the mind of the nameless protagonist

of Ralph Ellison's *Invisible Man*.
I lived in a tiny, turret-like room in the loft
of a drafty townhouse with a French violinist,

a librarian at Riker's Island,
and a German photographer, who cooked naked
while listening to Beethoven.

I loved to bike around the Coliseum and the Paterno
with a pregnant friend until the day I fainted
and while trying to revive me she fainted as well.

I read Chaucer and tossed it away,
then read it again. I inhaled Fanon, Danticat, Ondaatje.
At the Met, I saw Pissarro's *Washerwoman at Eragny*

I saw Wangechi Mutu's diptychs of sacred humanoids
and wept. I listened to Dizzy Gillespie while trying to sleep
and stood up stunned in a dream of reverence and felt

my mind elongate inside my mind.
I went to the Cathedral of St. John the Divine
and made a mute prayer among the godheads (Baldwin and Coltrane),

In Morningside Park, when I woke up, I heard Spanish laughter.
Everywhere I went in the city, I knew I was trailed by the ghost
of buried rivers.

PARADISE

Girls walk by the side of the road, a cluster of bright patterns.

—*Teju Cole*

Chibok, North of Nigeria
North of the country, a road led to the desert.
Dust was the first sentence. The Sahara
was a white darkness in the distance,
and beyond it the glint of a great lake.
We drove past fields of ginger and wild purple onions.
There was a public garden and a ring of white egrets
around still water.
At a farm, we met famers who knew the stiff silk
and red heart muscle of watermelons.
They hold the fruits close to their ears and listen
to measure their own decay.
At an animal sanctuary, we met a donkey named Happiness.
She had rheumy black eyes and a silvery blaze on her forehead.
We drove past a little town that was named in a language
that was disappearing. We arrived at the city called Paradise.
Its gate and city walls were burnt in the last
century and rebuilt only in a dream. Praise the emptiness.
We were offered water from wells dug by men of the desert tribe.
The wells, we were told, are older than the country.
The desert was once a lake.
Sorrow has such beautiful wings.
Women in black sarongs gathered around the wells.
The lake was in their voices, it rose and fell as they sang.
In a dream, their children vanished.
When they woke, the children remain vanished.
The girls, in a near forest, I imagine, huddle together,
as in the nightmare of children, afraid of the dark.

In the far distance, valleys of sorghum, minarets, and the sepulchers of kings. Pray for mercy. Here, the desert will eat your child.

MAN RADIATING HAPPINESS

You are melancholy photographed in strobe light. You
look good. You are banjo with wood tufts. You
are baby wolf on the tar chair listening to Monk's "Ruby, My Dear"
and quietly, then not quietly, weeping.
Your mother said you remember the way a trumpet
remembers wind. You
are "Equinox" playing from a stereo on a windowsill in Brooklyn at 4 a.m.
or the corked ear listening in the dark. You
are the hymn in the throat of this city
that has tried but failed to kill you.
You are the cliff in the blue clefs of Coltrane changes. You
are blue, not the color, the horn cry.
History invented your name.
Do you know your name?
You wear your weary well and call it jazz.
Your dance is a desperate signaling for help.
You are the ancient spell in the room.
You are the shadow anointing the floor.
You are music without silence.
Music without silence, what are you
hiding?

IN SEARCH OF JAMES BALDWIN IN SENEGAL

I

I had vowed the eyes of my son would see the world.
On a ferry, the island rose before us like a brilliant specter.
Forts, castles, and their cannons. Old colonial houses
on a sand elevation, rings of *Borassus* trees, and polished black
stones on the embarkment.
The air smelled and tasted like pink Himalayan salt.
We passed fish restaurants and open-air markets of ornate masks
and a posse of sculpted figurines. White tourists milled about with cameras.
At the island's mosque, built in 1825, holy men
prayed against shipwrecks. In a courtyard near the ocean, colorful pirogues
carved from rosewood idled on white sand by a cottage. The owner,
a blind woman, told us her dreams were waves of children drowning.
We heard the cry of a flock of hawks circling overhead.
They flapped and flailed with anger. The beaks, sharp, curved
mandibles. Their eyes, an alertness encoded by centuries
of wild hunger. And the majesty of their feathers, hundred needle points
of quills crosshatched like the delicate latticework of honeycombs.
We were not looking at birds, but at an intelligence held aloft by wings.
Did the birds, I thought, pass along to their offspring from generation
to generation, what they saw happen on this island?
Early the next dawn, in the muteness of the world, we woke early, my son and I,
and went for a swim in the ocean. We splashed about in the water, but it was cold
and dark. The Atlantic felt like a small dark room someone had shut us in.
I heard heavy footsteps approaching us from the beach and turned to look.
It was nothing but wind. I could hear the panicked drum of my heart.
Something twirled inside the water and darted between
my legs like an arrow or like it was inside me, but it was invisible to me
and I was invisible to it too. I wanted to say to my child, "Child, the ghosts

are not our enemies. The patter of feet you hear is the hurry of the millions returning
to us before dusk." When Baldwin came to this shore, it was said, he looked up and saw
a bright white ship departing, and he knew he was inside it and he knew it was 400 years ago.
He ran back to his hotel room and did not come out for three days.

II

I had vowed the eyes of my son would see the world.
In Gorée, shirtless black boys were diving and somersaulting
into the ocean, shrieking with laughter. They lifted up into the air,
beloved by gravity, then the release, arms spread, entering the water's blue
like a crucifix. The sky was seeded with brightness.
On the beach, young men in soccer jerseys—Zinedine Zidane, Ibrahimovic,
Thierry Henry—played a brisk game, raising a spray of fine dust.
They jostled for the ball and called after a fast, diminutive star, "Messi! Messi!"
A group of teenage girls giggled, hopped, and zigzagged across squares
drawn on sand, playing hopscotch. A girl sat on the lap of her brother
who plaited her hair into ombre cornrows. An old woman in a yellow
garment and black shoulder-length veil flew a kite. Children crowded
around her and tickled her. Her laughter was the laughter of her dead sister.
When Baldwin came here in 1947 with his sister, Gloria, he wrote
of how at the airport children wriggled out of their mother's embrace and ran
to him, thinking he was father or uncle. The crown of his desire:
To exist in the world as the opposite of panic. To be among a people
who anoint you kin by instinct. We chomped on ice cream, my son and I,
and walked through narrow alleyways between colonial buildings
with turquoise wooden windows and clay pots of red hibiscus and bougainvillea.
Lithe, sphinxlike cats—coal black with green eyes—leapt out of gardens.
Then we arrived at Maison des Esclaves, built in 1776.
It was pastel mud red with two staircases that curved downward elegantly.
Like the house of a benign grandfather. An archway led to shadowy basement
cells and a narrow stone door silhouetted against the ocean.
In one of those cells, we were shown rusted shackles, the color of dried blood,
coffles, chains, and whips for the enslaved. I reached out my hand and clasped it
around my son's eyes. No, I tried to clasp my hands around his eyes, but it was too late.
He had seen it. My lips were quivering. What was I trying to protect him from?
The heaviness in the room was like the heaviness of God's remorse.
Yet, outside, the brightness was undiminished
and we could still hear the laughter of the diving boys.

VOWS

Here, a memory: When my father fell
into himself and the waters

within him broke their
vows She

wilted to half of her carp.
She wrapped herself in a black shawl. She,

my mother, crawled
to his side, put her

ear to his chest. Said: if a body
is yours, you

can hear the needle of silence
its skin. She,

my mother, put her mouth
to my father's ear,

said I'll call your body,
which is mine, by name,

you'll come back to me.
How can a body the whole length

of which you once
traveled with your tongue close itself to you.

When he, my father, closed his eyes

and breath and his body became

a bridge he had left behind on a journey and
they wheeled him down the stairs,

she, my mother, sprang after them.
She cried out:

My name is
inside his tongue. I need to get it back.

VANISHING

I give you my rain,

the verbs and clatter from which there is no returning.

I give you my siren, my hymns, my psalms.

I give you maps, the crevice from which my cities have fallen.

I give you the small country of my laughter.

I give you lights parsing through lives, the fleeting

moth of days, my hours of beseeching.

I give you my private animals.

I give you the night hours from which I wake a city of salt.

PRAISE

(Ijala)

Blade of my century,
        praise
the flat ennui of the palm
        praise
feral indigo of my childhood
        praise
the prayers of my father
who is now a fossil
        praise.
I was taught the testament
and I knew the testament
        praise
language, theatre of trance,
antiphonal need
        praise
memory, light of memory
inside me
        praise
caesura of my breath
        praise

GORÉE

Shirtless black boys were diving and somersaulting
into the ocean, shrieking with laughter.

An old woman in a yellow garment and black shoulder-length veil
was flying a kite. Children crowded around her and tickled her.

Her laughter was not the laughter of her dead sister.
Baldwin came here in 1947 with his sister, Gloria,

to exist in the world, he said, as the opposite of panic.
To be among a people who anoint you kin by instinct.

At the island's mosque, built in 1825, holy men prayed,
but not against shipwrecks. There were no shipwrecks in human

language or history. In a courtyard near the ocean, there were colorful
pirogues carved
from rosewood and painted by a blind woman who told us

her dreams were never waves of children drowning. Children
never drowned or died face down in black dirt

or ruin or rubble. On this shore, Baldwin saw a bright white ship
and knew it was just that, a bright white ship, a cargo of mint and lotus.

ENVOY TO THE SOUTH OF FRANCE

Begin with the scene in Karen Thorsen's film *The Price of the Ticket*.
Begin with a seventeenth century, twelve-room stone house in the French
village, Saint-Paul de Vence, and its twenty-eight windows that open
to a view of a rose garden, the black licorice scent of olive groves,
a swarm of blue monarchs, and the Mediterranean Sea.
Inside that room, it was 1987 and James Baldwin was dying.
He was on a panel bed with a red quilt. His arms and legs throbbing
and aching, his beautiful fingers were arthritic, his lungs weak and
filled with fluid. They said he spoke in whispers. He said he was thirsty.
He said he wanted a feast of bread, butter, and salami.
His body in that state was like a still life painting.
Beauty in arrested motion.
Three men nursed him. Lucien Happersberger, a Swiss painter, his lover;
Bernard Hassell, a dancer and his confidante; and David, his younger brother.
They washed him. It must have felt like a ritual dance. They
began with the face—the face is the house of spirits—closing his eyes
with the soft pad of their fingertips. Then a dab of a moist washcloth
on his forehead and cheeks in a slow, circular motion.
Then his neck, then his chest. They were gentle, seeking
to protect the integrity of his skin.
They were waiting with him at a fragile door and did not know how far
they could go with him. One put his finger inside a bowl of clean water
and dripped it on Baldwin's lips lest he should be thirsty on his flight
to the Black heaven. Or perhaps, it was suddenly and briefly 1949
And Baldwin is young and wild again and he's back
in that room in Paris where he wrote *Giovanni's Room*.
All journeys are extraordinary, he once wrote in a letter.
I see him. I see a mirror. He turns and faces it.
He's combing and parting his hair, fingers adorned with rings.
He's watching himself in the mirror, that wicked gap-toothed smile.
Duke Ellington's *In a Sentimental Mood* is playing. He's swaying gently now.

He winks at us, and ready at last, turns toward that great door of return,
glides along the ancestral passageway and crosses it
with celestial swagger.

ELEGY OF HANDS

It is that my hands
are also my father's hands,

and where the lines meet on the palm
both of us have met

and sat, each with his own silence
not speaking.

It is not that we are fighting
It is the shape of love we have come to.

He keeping to his script of being dead
and I, doing the pose of the living in retaliation.

It is the shape of love we have come to.
On my way to the train this morning,

I cut through a small field of elms
and birches and thought I saw from afar

a white cluster, a crown of egrets
that had landed on the ground.

But really it was a cemetery.
It was as though the gravestones were holding hands.

It was the kind of thing that would have made him laugh:
gravestones holding hands.

I say this to him as

he sits beside me

And yes, he laughs.
He reaches out his hands toward me.

I pretend to not see the hands
I keep to the pose of the living.

ACKNOWLEDGMENTS

MANY THANKS TO the editors of the following journals, in which these poems have appeared, sometimes in slightly different versions:

Academy of American Poets' Poem-a-Day: "Glory"
Action, Spectacle: "Man Radiating Happiness"
Brooklyn Poets: "Citizen"
Guernica: "Brief History"
Harvard Review: "Elegy of Hands"
Narrative: "Death Does Not End at the Sea (A Sequence)"
Narrative: "I Carried My Father Across the Sea"
Narrative: "Vows"
Paris Review and *The Best American Poetry 2025*: "The People's History of 1998"
Palette Poetry: "Surrender"
Split This Rock: "Paradise"
Vinyl: "Vanishing"
Yale Review: "The Lovers of Modena"

I'm listening to Lokua Kanza's "Famille" as I write this. My heart is a sea. It swells with gratitude. I'm stunned by the fact that I now have a book in the world. It's a dream almost as old as my mind. Like a child sitting outside the door of a glass house, looking in with yearning, a little fear, and wonder. I'm still unable to shake the sense of wonder.

I thank my parents: My father, who was a model of language, erudition, and prayers. *Death is not silence. It's where I hear you most clearly*. My mother, my spring of confidence, my backing. Thank you for your wisdom. My siblings: Toyin, Tomiwa, Tobi, and Mayowa, my first chorus, my first artistic commune. May our chorus never break apart.

For years, I did not have teachers. I yearned for them, I prayed for them.

Kwame Dawes (for that email that changed things a decade ago and for that call last year), the late great Meena Alexander, Natalie Diaz, Gregory Pardlo (who taught me steadiness of craft and life, and how to dance with and against family history), Bernadine Evaristo and Kwame Dawes, again (for believing we, too, have a place in the chorus of diasporas), Sharon Olds, Major Jackson, Terrance Hayes (who taught me the discipline of dreaming, deep play, and creative restlessness), Meghan O'Rourke, Maaza Mengiste, Peter Balakian, Erica C. Doyle, James Kimbrell, Chris Okonkwo, Celia Caputi, and L. Lamar Wilson. Thank you all for your kindness. And of course the great Yusef Komunyakaa, for mystery.

I thank Alyson and Marc Adler (and Pretzel), who have always supported me, and for Valley Forge, which you made a refuge.

My commune at NYU and New York: Mimi, Anchal, Nadra, B, India and Ananda (my favs!), Karisma, Lola, Omotara, Madam Cordett, Susan Abraham, Doyin, Kemi, Yetunde, Mummy Godswill, Daddy Godswill, and Godswill (my boy!).

My commune and friends at Colgate and Hamilton: Peter, Jennifer, CJ, Ndinda, and my dear friend, Manuela. Thank you for friendship and community.

My commune and friends at FSU and Tallahassee: the marvelous Esther Ifesinachi Okonkwo (for all the long drives and laughter), and dear Hera Naguib who saw early versions of this project, told me there was something beautiful there and cheered me on. My main man, Eddie Hearne, my brother, Vincent and Crys. Landis, for everything. My dear brother and friend, Tosin Theophilus, his wonderful wife, and their children for being my family when I was far away from family. The MFM Tallahassee family: Pastor Adeniyi and his family, and everyone. Thank you for community.

My friends and commune at JMU and Harrisonburg: Nikema Bells, Evangel Olujide (àbúró mi dáadáa, osé ganni o), Mercy (àwọn tèmi nílé lóko), Case Watkins and Kristine Wylie and their lovely daughters, Femi, Jimi, Toks, Excellence, the Ijeluolas, Professor Adérónké Adésànyà (Mama the mama!), Thandwa, Ololade, James, Emmanuel, and others.

The institutions that have supported me and helped me do my work all these years: the Norman Mailer Center, Fine Arts Work Center, Provincetown, Poet's House, New York, New York University, Colgate University, Florida State University, the Schomburg Center for Research in Black Culture, the Woodberry Poetry Room and Houghton Rare Books and Manuscript Library at Harvard University, the Folger Shakespeare Library, Washington DC, James Madison University, and the Furious Flower Poetry Center. Dr. Joanne Gabbin and Lauren K. Alleyne.

Siwar Masannat and Jessica Pool at *Prairie Schooner*. Katrina Vassallo, Courtney Ochsner, and everyone at University of Nebraska Press for your kind work on this book. My people at *A Long House*. Kechi, Yinka, Joseph, Clarie, and our editorial fellows.

My students everywhere (at NYU, Colgate, FSU, JMU, Brooklyn Poets). Thank you all for the magical spaces we made together. I still believe poetry is the eloquence of what is veiled by history. I still believe poetry, as Audrey Lorde taught us, is not luxury.

Before this beginning, there was another beginning: Ibukun Adeeko, Opeyemi, Nurain, Jibosky, Tope Olaifa, Baba Olanipekun, ANA Abeokuta, Niyi Osundare, et al.

Before that beginning, there was another one: *The three Sages! Yemi Adesina*, O.O.J. (we dreamt of this together), Tope Apoola, Asake Busayo (ọrun re ẹ o, pàdí mi). CAC Oke Ipadabo where the seed of the word was sown. Bro Dotun and Bro Sam. Elder Ariyo, Elder Owolafe, Mama Badiora. Àwa ni ìmọ̀lè ayé, ìlú ta tẹ̀dó sórí òkè kò le farasin.

Yemisi, àbúró mi dáadáa. Fikky Mama, Shenexy Baba and family (especially my godson). Hauwa, for voice notes and laughter. Joy Priest, for laughter and poems. You saw what was there. I'm definitely leaving out some incredible people. But there'll be more books.

I'm listening to Cesaria Evora's "Sodade." My heart is full. Àwa ni ìmọ̀lè ayé. Ẹ̀sé modúpẹ́.

IN THE RAZ/SHUMAKER PRAIRIE SCHOONER
BOOK PRIZE IN POETRY SERIES

To order or obtain more information on these or other University of Nebraska
Press titles, visit nebraskapress.unl.edu.

www.ingramcontent.com/pod-product-compliance
Ingram Content Group UK Ltd.
Pitfield, Milton Keynes, MK11 3LW, UK
UKHW041917251125
465350UK00005B/436